A Light to the World

A Light to the World

Reflections from Kylemore Abbey

COLUMBA

First published in 2009 by

the columba press

55A Spruce Avenue, Stillorgan Industrial Park, Blackrock, Co Dublin

Designed by Bill Bolger
Photography by Neil Warner
Additional photography by
Tony O'Connell, Sr Noreen Gallagher, Trish Monaghan, Pavol Seregi.
Printed in Ireland by Watermans, Cork

ISBN 978-1-85607-570-1

Acknowledgements
Scripture quotations are from the *New Revised Standard Version*, copyright © 1989
by the Division of Christian Education of the National Council of the Churches
of Christ in the United States of America. Used by permission.

A Light to the World

Praying the psalms in Kylemore

This little prayer book contains many of the prayers recited and meditated by the Benedictine nuns of Kylemore Abbey, and it invites you to join them occasionally or often, from afar, as they gather in the chapel for their daily prayer of praise, thanksgiving and intercession.

The nuns come together every day of the year early in the morning, at midday, in the evening and at fall of night, to pray and sing the psalms. The Book of Psalms consists of 150 poetic prayers, composed in and around Jerusalem roughly between the years 1000 and 500 before Christ.

Why pray out of ancient books? If I want to pray, is it not better to pray from my own heart, responding to my own situation? Yes, but very many people find that although they may want to pray, praying does not come naturally. The Book of Psalms has been regarded since it was first put together not just as a book of texts with which to pray and praise God, but as a kind of school of prayer, a book through which one discovers what prayer is, and learns how to do it, sooner or later breaking out into one's own unique form of prayer.

The people who composed the psalms were Jews who believed profoundly that God was in their lives. He was the Creator of the world, and the Creator of each one of them personally. He had revealed himself first to Abraham, and had called him to leave his own country and move to the land we now call Israel. Later, when the Israelites moved to Egypt because of a famine and were enslaved there, it was God who inspired Moses to lead them out of slavery and back to their own land. God remains a mystery to us, immeasurably beyond the limitations of our understanding, but he is constantly making his love and his presence felt. As Creator, he is present through his Creation. He loves the human beings he has made and wants them to grow to fullness of life. He protects them and sends them comfort in all the pains and problems that life brings. He helps them in every need. The psalms are poems, poetic outpourings, of people who have sensed or experienced his presence in nature, in history, in themselves, and want to respond to him. They are songs of praise for the wonder of the world. They express thanks for God's goodness and guidance. They are cries for help in need, sickness and distress. They are expressions of fear and desolation in the face of death. They are the responses of man and woman to experiences that have the quality of universality, experiences that are not limited to any time or any culture, but that are shared by all human beings at all times.

The Book of Psalms is a school of prayer, because it helps and teaches people of any century and in any part of the world to find words to express their religious feelings. One learns to pray with the psalms, first by getting familiar with some words of the psalmist and making them one's own, and from there on, learning, if one wants to, to use one's very own, personal words. Many people move on from praying with words into a deep, wordless prayer. Benedictine nuns and monks, and many other people too, spend their lives in this school of prayer. Learners in this school make progress not by knowing all the psalms by heart, not by knowing a lot about their history, but by learning through them to be aware of the presence of God all around them, and to be reaching out to him from the depths of their being, with their own words, or in their own silence. It is a school in which one never finishes learning. It goes on forever.

The nuns of Kylemore, like nuns and monks of the Catholic and Orthodox Churches and many others too, follow the ancient practice of praying all 150 of these psalms within a particular space of time. The ancient monks in the desert of Egypt and Palestine prayed all 150 psalms each day. St Benedict introduced a moderate reform of monastic life in Europe in the sixth century, and extended the time for praying the 150 psalms from one day to one week. In our time, the Order recommends various different ways of following this practice, leaving it to the individual communities to decide what is best for themselves – two weeks, or a month, or longer. There are some psalms that are traditionally linked with the liturgical seasons and feasts – Advent, Christmas, Lent, Easter, Pentecost. The rest are spread out over 'ordinary time', the times in the liturgical year, winter, spring, summer and autumn that are simply focused on living the Christian faith in everyday life.

How do I learn to pray the psalms?

Since much of the poetry of the psalms has gone into the literary, musical and religious culture of western Europe, it is not unlikely that some psalm verses are already familiar to you, for instance: 'The Lord is my shepherd' (Psalm 23) or 'The heavens declare the glory of the Lord' (Psalm 19) or 'My God, my God, why have you forsaken me?' (Psalm 22). Such verses may at some time or another have spoken to you, or struck you as having something to do with your own life. Learning to pray with the psalms involves reading them in such a way that the mind and heart are open to being touched in a similar manner.

You can start reading any psalm at random. The Rule of St Benedict begins with the word 'Listen', and this applies to reading the sacred scriptures. We read them not in the way in which we are used to reading, looking for information, pleasure or entertainment. We read them in a listening mode, quietly attentive to the words, and listening for what the author is saying to us. So you read on in the psalm you have chosen with this attentiveness, until something touches or moves you. You read: 'Be still and know that I am God' (Psalm 46), and you sense in the depths of your heart a longing to turn down the noise of everyday life, and just be quiet, listening for the reality beyond the sounds of the world. 'I will sing to the Lord all my life, make music to my God while I live' (Psalm 104) could touch you with joy in the world and creation, and a longing to express that joy and your gratitude for it. 'If the Lord does not build the house, they labour in vain who build' (127) might move you with a sense of the precariousness of all human endeavours, and the sustainable reliability of the Creator who is guiding the world and ourselves to its goal.

You then accept a certain ownership of that verse, repeating it and savouring it, allowing it to touch still deeper associations in your heart or your life-story. You may find that you are learning verses by heart, like lines of a poem. You remember that God is present to you, and you may feel drawn to addressing the words of the psalm to him, or moving from the words of the psalm into words of your own. After a while, you return to the psalm you were reading, and read on until another verse touches your heart, and you repeat the steps of listening, repeating, speaking to God. Some people practise this psalm-prayer in an informal way, others like to give it an order of its own, choosing a fixed length of time for it and maybe a fixed time of day and a special place.

With time and practice, psalm verses, and then whole psalms, become part of the furnishings of your inner sanctuary, enabling you to move relatively easily into prayer, whatever your state of mind or your mood. Jesus prayed the psalms in this way, and the gospels tell us of several situations in which a psalm verse gives him the words he needs to communicate with the Father.

If you like this book and use it occasionally or often as a prayer-book, please remember then the nuns of Kylemore, and know they are praying with you and for you and all of those you care for.

Mitchell Henry

Among the visitors to Connemara in the 1840s was a wealthy English doctor, Mitchell Henry, son of an Irish industrialist who had built up a successful textile business in Manchester. In September 1849 Mitchell Henry, with his young wife Margaret, spent part of their honeymoon in Connemara, staying maybe at Kylemore House, where a Dublin man, Andrew Armstrong, ran a hotel. The opening of the Great Western Railway Dublin–Galway in 1851 made Connemara more accessible to tourists, and Mitchell Henry became one of the growing number of Irish and English gentlemen who visited the area during the fishing season. In the peace of the secluded pass, he relaxed from his busy life in his Harley Street practice and as a lecturer in Medicine at the Middlesex Hospital Medical College. It is possible that he rented Kylemore Lodge for these visits, a fishing lodge built by Rev Robert Isaac Wilberforce after 1853 on the shore of Lake Pollacappul at the foot of Duchruach Mountain.

In 1862 his father died, leaving a large fortune to be divided among his

children and grandchildren, and Mitchell Henry became a wealthy man. He changed his lifestyle, and gave up his medical career in London. He moved back to Manchester to take over his deceased father's business and to become involved in politics. At the same time he could now afford to develop his interest in art and culture. In 1863 he purchased Stratheden House in Knightsbridge, London, and fitted and furnished it elaborately with collectors' items, making it over the years a showcase for the many treasures he and his wife had acquired and the influences they had experienced. He had taken a lease on Kylemore Lodge in 1862 and purchased it in 1864, possibly at first simply with a view to having a holiday home in the region he had become so attached to.

A Unitarian by education and persuasion, he had been formed in an ethos of hard work, liberalism in politics, tolerance in religion, and responsibility of the wealthy to alleviate the lot of the poor. Cross Street Chapel, the meeting place of the Unitarian community in Manchester, was in the 19th century a centre of social reform. Mitchell Henry had grown up in an environment concerned to improve the living conditions of the poor

and to expand their educational opportunities. He was not a man to spend his wealth simply on selfish luxury. He saw it as a gift which would leave him free to devote himself to building up a better world. He believed, as a Unitarian, that the poor should be empowered not only to keep pace with the rapid changes in society brought about by technological advancement, but also to open their hearts to beauty in art, culture and the humble events of daily life.

His decision to replace Kylemore Lodge with a spectacular castle was not the whim of a capitalist looking for new playthings, nor was it even, as the legends that have grown up around Kylemore maintain, simply to satisfy a romantic wish of his wife Margaret. During his first visits to Kylemore, Connemara was still suffering in the aftermath of the potato famine (1845-1852). Poverty, undernourishment, sickness, lack of education and skills, unemployment dominated the lives of the people. Mitchell Henry's plan for Kylemore was to enhance the natural beauty of the place with beauty that is the work of human hands - a stunning building with a spectacular garden and a modern working farm, all set in an estate that was being developed and cared for to the benefit of the impoverished region. It was not just to be a delightful family home, but also a place to provide employment to men and women of the area, and to teach them work and social skills that would give them some hope of independence and improvement.

Building began in 1867 and ended in 1871. In the following year, Margaret gave birth to the 9th child of the marriage, so that Kylemore with its gardens and estate was housing, at least for part of the year, a large family plus the staff and servants necessary for this ménage, including frequent visitors. Once the building was completed, Mitchell resumed the political activities he had briefly pursued in England 1862-1867, and in 1871 he stood as a liberal candidate for the by-election in Galway for the Irish Nationalists of the Home Rule League. After his election in 1871, he worked tirelessly in the House of Commons to defend Irish interests and gain respect for Irish causes.

This privileged family life was shattered after only 3 years in Kylemore by

the death of Margaret, aged 45, on a holiday with the family in Egypt. Her remains were brought back to Kylemore and laid to rest in a Mausoleum which her husband built for her near the east gate of the castle. The exquisite neo-Gothic chapel which he erected in her memory 4 years later is a tender witness to their relationship. Mitchell never recovered from the loss of his beloved wife. He continued his political career, and spent some time every year in Kylemore with the younger children, but the optimistic spirit with which he had launched out on his new life in 1862 was broken.

A further tragedy struck in 1892 when his daughter Geraldine was killed in an accident on the road near the Castle. By now his finances had fallen into disarray due to unfortunate investments, and in 1893 he was obliged to put Kylemore up for sale. He left the place, never to return, and the Castle he had built was finally sold in 1902. He died in Leamington in England in 1910. His ashes were brought back to Kylemore and placed beside Margaret's in the Mausoleum. In 1903 the new owner, the Duke of Manchester and his wife, moved in.

Their mortgage was foreclosed upon in 1913, and the house was finally resold in 1920 to the Irish Dames of Ypres.

The Benedictine Nuns of Kylemore

A detailed history of the Benedictine Community of Kylemore can be read in Kathleen Villiers-Tuthill's book 'History of Kylemore Abbey and Castle', Kylemore Abbey Publications 2002, from which the following is summarised.

The community was founded in Ypres, Flanders, in 1665, by a group of English Benedictines from the Abbey of Ghent, led by Dame Marina Beaumont. Due to the laws aimed at rooting out the practice of the Catholic faith (Penal Laws), it was difficult at that time for religious houses to survive either in England or in Ireland. Lady Abbess Marina was joined shortly by some Irish postulants, and within a few years the monastery in Ypres (Monastery of the Immaculate Conception of the Blessed Virgin Mary Gratia Dei) became officially the Irish Benedictine house on the

continent. With the encouragement of King James II, an attempt was made in 1688 to set up a foundation in Dublin, but after the defeat at the Battle of the Boyne, the founding nuns returned to Ypres. For well over 250 years the community continued to live there, with the purpose of providing an education and a religious community for Irish women. During that time, the Abbey attracted the daughters of the Irish nobility, both as students and as nuns, and enjoyed the patronage of many influential Irish families living in exile. Nano Nagle, foundress of the Irish Presentation Sisters, may have been one of their pupils.

The Rule of St Benedict teaches the Christian way to holiness – a contemplative journey on which the monk or nun learns the virtues of respect for Creation and tradition, hard work, simplicity, respect and love for the people one lives with, openness and hospitality to strangers, and patience and trust in God in the face of the adversities of life. The goal of the journey is Christ. He too is the way and the light that illumines and encourages. The practice of prayer, including the daily prayer of the psalms, is the ambience in which this contemplative life burgeons and puts down roots. The history of the Benedictine nuns of Ypres for almost two and a half centuries mirrors this contemplative journey, culminating in their survival after the destruction of the monastery in the bombing of Ypres during the First World War.

Soon after the outbreak of the war in October 1914, the monastery was completely gutted by fire. The nuns had to flee from Belgium. They found temporary homes in Poperinge (Flanders), then in Oulton (Staffordshire, England), and London. The Irish Abbot of the Belgian Benedictine monastery of Maredsous, Columba Marmion, encouraged them to take the momentous step of attempting a return to Ireland. For four years they lived in Macmine, Co Wexford, but the house there proved too small for the needs of the community and their school. Finally, on November 30th 1920, with the War of Independence in all its brutality still being fought out, the nuns moved to Kylemore Castle in Connemara, to continue their contemplative journey there.

The community's presence proved, from the time of their arrival, to be a blessing for the locality. The nuns brought to this remote region knowledge and expertise which they used for the education of girls, the employment of workers, and later for the building up of Kylemore as a unique centre of welcome in Ireland, restoring and maintaining buildings and gardens, and sparing nothing in order to offer visitors from all over the world an unforgettable experience.

In 2004 it was decided to close the school. The phasing-out is due to be completed in 2010. Kylemore is by now known all over the world, and the community sees its outreach for the next stage of its existence not in the school but in the service of hospitality to former students and to all other visitors who come. The nuns continue on the Christian contemplative journey with the Gospel and the Rule of St. Benedict as guide, singing day by day the psalms from which their monastic mothers for hundreds of years learned the way of life.

Listen

Psalm 46 Be Still

God is our refuge and strength,
a very present help in trouble.
Therefore we will not fear, though the earth should change,
though the mountains shake in the heart of the sea.

Though its waters roar and foam,
though the mountains tremble with its tumult,
God is in the midst of the city; it shall not be moved;
God will help it when the morning dawns.

Come, behold the works of the Lord:
'Be still, and know that I am God!
I am exalted among the nations,
I am exalted in the earth.'

Psalm 104 *(part one)*

Praise the Lord, the loving Creator

Bless the Lord, O my soul.
O Lord my God, you are very great.
You are clothed with honour and majesty,
wrapped in light as with a garment.

You stretch out the heavens like a tent,
you set the beams of your chambers on the waters,
you make the clouds your chariot,
you ride on the wings of the wind,
you make the winds your messengers,
fire and flame your ministers.

You set the earth on its foundations,
so that it shall never be shaken.
You cover it with the deep as with a garment;
the waters stood above the mountains.

Psalm 104 *continued*

You make springs gush forth in the valleys;
they flow between the hills,
giving drink to every wild animal;
the wild asses quench their thirst.
By the streams the birds of the air have
       their habitation;
they sing among the branches.
From your lofty abode you water
      the mountains;
the earth is satisfied with the fruit of
      your work.

You cause the grass to grow for the cattle,
and plants for people to use,
to bring forth food from the earth,
and wine to gladden the human heart,
oil to make the face shine,
and bread to strengthen the human heart.
The trees of the Lord are watered abundantly,
the cedars of Lebanon that he planted.
In them the birds build their nests;
the stork has its home in the fir trees.
The high mountains are for the wild goats;
the rocks are a refuge for the coneys.

Psalm 104 *continued*

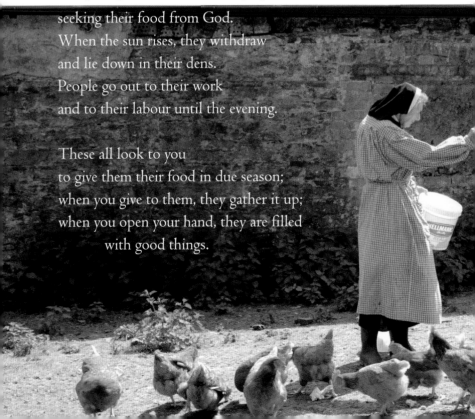

You have made the moon to mark the seasons;
the sun knows its time for setting.
You make darkness, and it is night,
when all the animals of the forest come creeping out.
The young lions roar for their prey,
seeking their food from God.
When the sun rises, they withdraw
and lie down in their dens.
People go out to their work
and to their labour until the evening.

These all look to you
to give them their food in due season;
when you give to them, they gather it up;
when you open your hand, they are filled
with good things.

I will sing to the Lord as long as I live;
I will sing praise to my God while I have being.
May my meditation be pleasing to him,
for I rejoice in the Lord.
Bless the Lord, O my soul.

Psalm 8   *In his own image and likeness*

O Lord, our Sovereign,
how majestic is your name in all the earth!

You have set your glory above the heavens.
Out of the mouths of babes and infants
you have founded a bulwark because of your foes,
to silence the enemy and the avenger.

When I look at your heavens, the work of your fingers,
the moon and the stars that you have established;
what are human beings that you are mindful of them,
mortals that you care for them?

Yet you have made them a little lower than God,
and crowned them with glory and honour.
You have given them dominion over the works of your hands;
you have put all things under their feet,
all sheep and oxen,
and also the beasts of the field,
the birds of the air, and the fish of the sea,
whatever passes along the paths of the seas.
Lord, our Sovereign, how majestic is your name in all the earth!

Winter – Advent
– Christmas
– Ordinary Time

Psalm 2 God's Promise

Why do the nations conspire,
and the peoples plot in vain?
The kings of the earth set themselves,
and the rulers take counsel together,
against the Lord and his anointed, saying,
'Let us burst their bonds asunder,
and cast their cords from us.'
He who sits in the heavens laughs;
the Lord has them in derision.
Then he will speak to them in his wrath,
and terrify them in his fury, saying,
'I have set my king on Zion, my holy hill.'

Psalm 2 *continued*

I will tell of the decree of the Lord:
He said to me, 'You are my son;
today I have begotten you.
Ask of me, and I will make the nations your heritage,
and the ends of the earth your possession.
You shall break them with a rod of iron,
and dash them in pieces like a potter's vessel.'

Now therefore, O kings, be wise;
be warned, O rulers of the earth.
Serve the Lord with fear,
with trembling kiss his feet,
or he will be angry, and you will perish in the way;
for his wrath is quickly kindled.

Happy are all who take refuge in him.

Psalm 24　See, I stand at the gate and knock

The earth is the Lord's and all that is in it,
the world, and those who live in it;
for he has founded it on the seas,
and established it on the rivers.

Lift up your heads, O gates!
and be lifted up, O ancient doors!
that the King of glory may come in.
Who is the King of glory?
The Lord, strong and mighty,
the Lord, mighty in battle.
Lift up your heads, O gates!
and be lifted up, O ancient doors!
that the King of glory may come in.
Who is this King of glory?
The Lord of hosts,
he is the King of glory.

Luke 1:68-79 *Benedictus*

Blessed be the Lord God of Israel,

for he has looked favourably on his people and redeemed them.

He has raised up a mighty saviour for us

in the house of his servant David,

as he spoke through the mouth of his holy prophets from of old,

that we would be saved from our enemies and from the hand of all
        who hate us.

Thus he has shown the mercy promised to our ancestors,

and has remembered his holy covenant,

the oath that he swore to our ancestor Abraham,

to grant us that we, being rescued from the hands of our enemies,

might serve him without fear, in holiness and righteousness
        before him all our days.

And you, child, will be called the prophet of the Most High;

for you will go before the Lord to prepare his ways,

to give knowledge of salvation to his people

by the forgiveness of their sins.

By the tender mercy of our God,

the dawn from on high will break upon us,

to give light to those who sit in darkness and in the shadow of death,

to guide our feet into the way of peace.'

Psalm 15 *Walk in his ways*

O Lord, who may abide in your tent?
Who may dwell on your holy hill?

Those who walk blamelessly, and do what is right,
and speak the truth from their heart;
who do not slander with their tongue,
and do no evil to their friends,
nor take up a reproach against their neighbours;
in whose eyes the wicked are despised,
but who honour those who fear the Lord;
who stand by their oath even to their hurt;
who do not lend money at interest,
and do not take a bribe against the innocent.

Those who do these things shall never be moved.

Mitchell Henry, see Introduction page 11.

Psalm 141 *Set a guard over my mouth*

I call upon you, O Lord; come quickly to me;
give ear to my voice when I call to you.
Let my prayer be counted as incense before you,
and the lifting up of my hands as an evening sacrifice.

Set a guard over my mouth, O Lord;
keep watch over the door of my lips.
Do not turn my heart to any evil,
to busy myself with wicked deeds
in company with those who work iniquity;
do not let me eat of their delicacies.

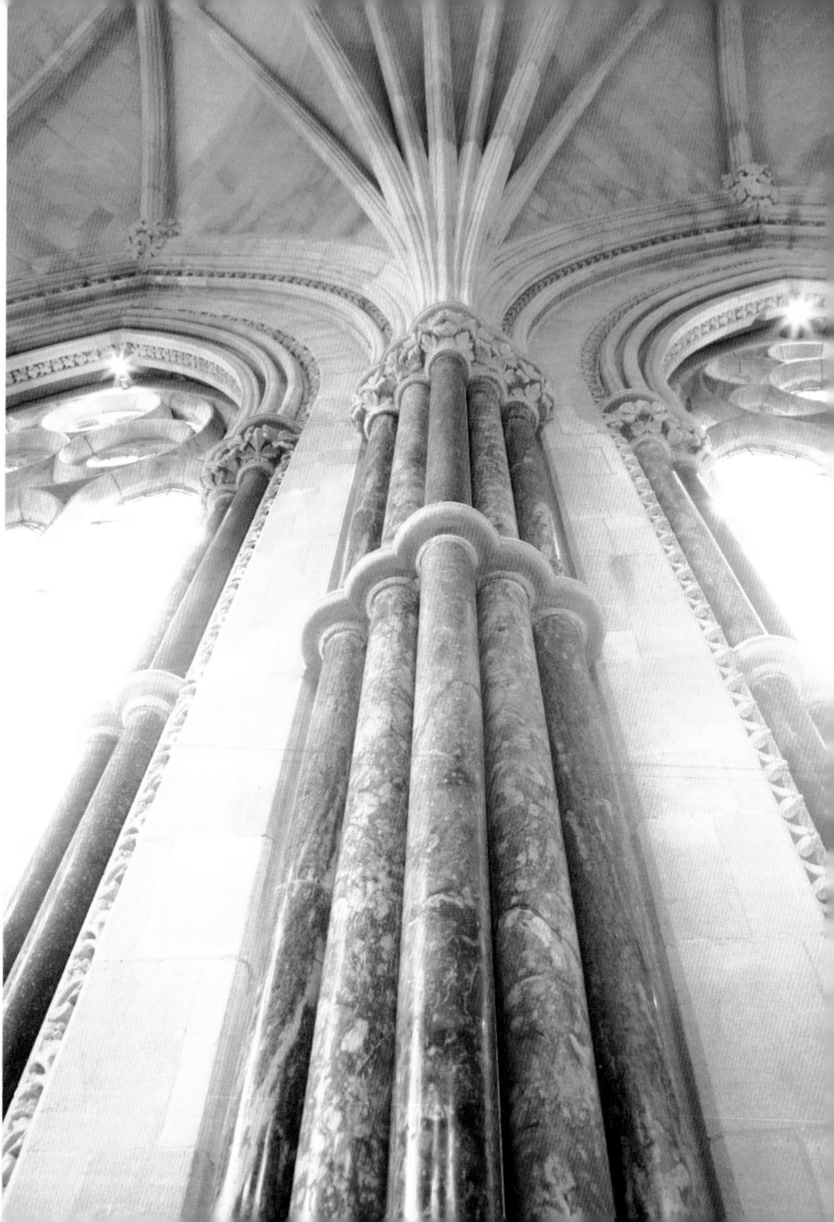

Psalm 144 *(beginning at verse 9)*

Thanks for health and happiness

I will sing a new song to you, O God;
upon a ten-stringed harp I will play to you,
the one who gives victory to kings,
who rescues his servant David.
Rescue me from the cruel sword,
and deliver me from the hand of aliens,
whose mouths speak lies,
and whose right hands are false.

> May our sons in their youth
> be like plants full grown,
> our daughters like corner pillars,
> cut for the building of a palace.
> May our barns be filled
> with produce of every kind;
> may our sheep increase by thousands,
> by tens of thousands in our fields,
> and may our cattle be heavy with young.
> May there be no breach in the walls, no exile,
> and no cry of distress in our streets.

Happy are the people to whom such blessings fall;
happy are the people whose God is the Lord.

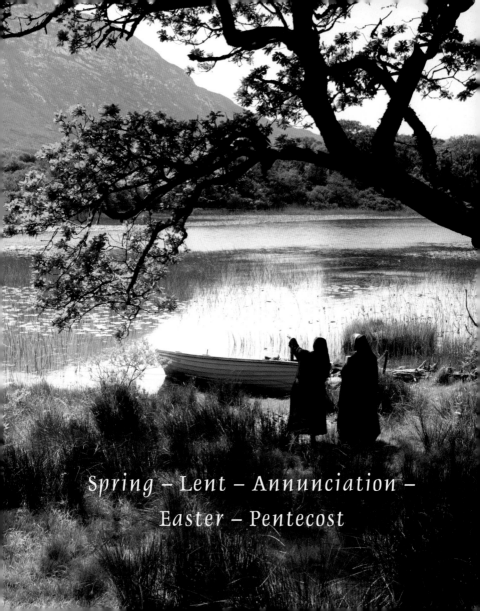

Spring – Lent – Annunciation –
Easter – Pentecost

Psalm 63 *Longing for God*

God, you are my God, I seek you,
my soul thirsts for you;
my flesh faints for you,
as in a dry and weary land where there is no water.
So I have looked upon you in the sanctuary,
beholding your power and glory.
Because your steadfast love is better than life,
my lips will praise you.
So I will bless you as long as I live;
I will lift up my hands and call on your name.

My soul is satisfied as with a rich feast,
and my mouth praises you with joyful lips
when I think of you on my bed,
and meditate on you in the watches of the night;
for you have been my help,
and in the shadow of your wings I sing for joy.
My soul clings to you;
your right hand upholds me.

Psalm 25 *Make me know your ways*

To you, O Lord, I lift up my soul.
O my God, in you I trust;
do not let me be put to shame;

> Make me to know your ways, O Lord;
> teach me your paths.
> Lead me in your truth, and teach me,
> for you are the God of my salvation.

Good and upright is the Lord;
therefore he instructs sinners in the way.
He leads the humble in what is right,
and teaches the humble his way.

> All the paths of the Lord are steadfast love
>   and faithfulness,
> for those who keep his covenant and his decrees.
> They will abide in prosperity,
> and their children shall possess the land.
> The friendship of the Lord is for those who fear him,
> and he makes his covenant known to them.

Psalm 84 *Holy places*

How lovely is your dwelling place,
O Lord of hosts!
My soul longs, indeed it faints
for the courts of the Lord;
my heart and my flesh sing for joy
to the living God.

Even the sparrow finds a home,
and the swallow a nest for herself,
where she may lay her young,
at your altars, O Lord of hosts,
my King and my God.
Happy are those who live in your house,
ever singing your praise.
They go from strength to strength;
the God of gods will be seen in Zion.

For a day in your courts is better
than a thousand elsewhere.
I would rather be a doorkeeper in the house of my God
than live in the tents of wickedness.
For the Lord God is a sun and shield;
he bestows favour and honour.
No good thing does the Lord withhold
from those who walk uprightly.
Lord of hosts,
happy is everyone who trusts in you.

Luke 1:46-55 *Magnificat*

My soul magnifies the Lord,
and my spirit rejoices in God my Saviour,
for he has looked with favour on the lowliness of his servant.
Surely, from now on all generations will call me blessed;
for the Mighty One has done great things for me,
and holy is his name.
His mercy is for those who fear him
from generation to generation.
He has shown strength with his arm;
he has scattered the proud in the thoughts of their hearts.
He has brought down the powerful from their thrones,
and lifted up the lowly;
he has filled the hungry with good things,
and sent the rich away empty.
He has helped his servant Israel,
in remembrance of his mercy,
according to the promise he made to our ancestors,
to Abraham and to his descendants for ever.

Psalm 14 *Fools*

Fools say in their hearts, 'There is no God.'
They are corrupt, they do abominable deeds;
there is no one who does good.

> The Lord looks down from heaven on
> humankind
> to see if there are any who are wise,
> who seek after God.

They have all gone astray, they are all alike perverse;
there is no one who does good,
no, not one.

> Have they no knowledge, all the evildoers
> who eat up my people as they eat bread,
> and do not call upon the Lord?

There they shall be in great terror,
for God is with the company of the righteous.
You would confound the plans of the poor,
but the Lord is their refuge.

O that deliverance for Israel would come from Zion!
When the Lord restores the fortunes of his people,
Jacob will rejoice; Israel will be glad.

Praise and thanks for God's kindness

Bless the Lord, O my soul,
and all that is within me,
bless his holy name.
Bless the Lord, O my soul,
and do not forget all his benefits –
who forgives all your iniquity,
who heals all your diseases,
who redeems your life from the Pit,
who crowns you with steadfast love and mercy,
who satisfies you with good as long as you live
so that your youth is renewed like the eagle's.

The Lord is merciful and gracious,
slow to anger and abounding in steadfast love.
He will not always accuse,
nor will he keep his anger for ever.
He does not deal with us according to our sins,
nor repay us according to our iniquities.
For as the heavens are high above the earth,
so great is his steadfast love towards those who fear him;
as far as the east is from the west,
so far he removes our transgressions from us.

Psalm 103 *continued*

As a father has compassion for his children,
so the Lord has compassion for those who fear him.
For he knows how we were made;
he remembers that we are dust.

As for mortals, their days are like grass;
they flourish like a flower of the field;
for the wind passes over it, and it is gone,
and its place knows it no more.
But the steadfast love of the Lord is from
            everlasting to everlasting
on those who fear him,
and his righteousness to children's children,
to those who keep his covenant
and remember to do his commandments.

Bless the Lord, all his hosts,
his ministers that do his will.
Bless the Lord, all his works,
in all places of his dominion.
Bless the Lord, O my soul.

Prayer to God in darkness

My God, my God, why have you forsaken me?
Why are you so far from helping me, from the words of my groaning?
O my God, I cry by day, but you do not answer;
and by night, but find no rest.

Yet you are holy,
enthroned on the praises of Israel.
In you our ancestors trusted;
they trusted, and you delivered them.
To you they cried, and were saved;
in you they trusted, and were not put to shame.

But I am a worm, and not human;
scorned by others, and despised by the people.
All who see me mock at me;
they make mouths at me, they shake their heads;
Commit your cause to the Lord; let him deliver –
let him rescue the one in whom he delights.'

Yet it was you who took me from the womb;
you kept me safe on my mother's breast.
On you I was cast from my birth,
and since my mother bore me you have been my God.
Do not be far from me,
for trouble is near
and there is no one to help.

Psalm 118 *It is better to trust in the Lord than to trust in rulers*

O give thanks to the Lord, for he is good;
his steadfast love endures for ever!

Let Israel say,
'His steadfast love endures for ever.'

Out of my distress I called on the Lord;
the Lord answered me and set me in a broad place.
With the Lord on my side I do not fear.
What can mortals do to me?
The Lord is on my side to help me;
I shall look in triumph on those who hate me.
It is better to take refuge in the Lord
than to put confidence in mortals.
It is better to take refuge in the Lord
than to put confidence in princes.

'The right hand of the Lord does valiantly;
the right hand of the Lord is exalted;
the right hand of the Lord does valiantly.'

I shall not die, but I shall live,
and recount the deeds of the Lord.

The stone that the builders rejected
has become the chief cornerstone.
This is the Lord's doing;
it is marvellous in our eyes.
This is the day that the Lord has made;
let us rejoice and be glad in it.

Bind the festal procession with branches,
up to the horns of the altar.

You are my God, and I will give thanks to you;
you are my God, I will extol you.

O give thanks to the Lord, for he is good,
for his steadfast love endures for ever.

Psalm 19 *God, my Rock*

The heavens are telling the glory of God;
and the firmament proclaims his handiwork.
Day to day pours forth speech,
and night to night declares knowledge.
There is no speech, nor are there words;
their voice is not heard;
yet their voice goes out through all the earth,
and their words to the end of the world.

In the heavens he has set a tent for the sun,
which comes out like a bridegroom from his wedding canopy,
and like a strong man runs its course with joy.
Its rising is from the end of the heavens,
and its circuit to the end of them;
and nothing is hidden from its heat.

The law of the Lord is perfect,
reviving the soul;
the decrees of the Lord are sure,
making wise the simple.

Let the words of my mouth and the meditation of my heart
be acceptable to you,
O Lord, my rock and my redeemer.

Psalm 16 *Thanks to God for joy and hope*

Protect me, O God, for in you I take refuge.
I say to the Lord, 'You are my Lord;
I have no good apart from you.'

As for the holy ones in the land, they are the noble,
      in whom is all my delight.

The Lord is my chosen portion and my cup;
      you hold my lot.
The boundary lines have fallen for me in pleasant places;
I have a goodly heritage.

I bless the Lord who gives me counsel;
in the night also my heart instructs me.
I keep the Lord always before me;
      because he is at my right hand, I shall not be moved.

Therefore my heart is glad, and my soul rejoices;
      my body also rests secure.
For you do not give me up to Sheol,
or let your faithful one see the Pit.

You show me the path of life.
In your presence there is fullness of joy;
      in your right hand are pleasures for evermore.

Psalm 27 *One thing*

The Lord is my light and my salvation;
whom shall I fear?
The Lord is the stronghold of my life;
of whom shall I be afraid?

When evildoers assail me
to devour my flesh –
my adversaries and foes –
they shall stumble and fall.

Though an army encamp against me,
my heart shall not fear;
though war rise up against me,
yet I will be confident.
One thing I asked of the Lord,
that will I seek after:
to live in the house of the Lord
all the days of my life,
to behold the beauty of the Lord,
and to inquire in his temple.

For he will hide me in his shelter
in the day of trouble;
he will conceal me under the cover of his tent;
he will set me high on a rock.

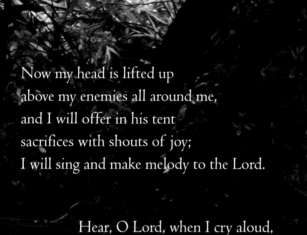

Now my head is lifted up
above my enemies all around me,
and I will offer in his tent
sacrifices with shouts of joy;
I will sing and make melody to the Lord.

Hear, O Lord, when I cry aloud,
be gracious to me and answer me!
'Come,' my heart says, 'seek his face!'
Your face, Lord, do I seek.
Do not hide your face from me.

Teach me your way, O Lord,
and lead me on a level path.
because of my enemies.

I believe that I shall see the goodness of the Lord
in the land of the living.
Wait for the Lord;
be strong, and let your heart take courage;
wait for the Lord!

Do not turn your servant away in anger,
you who have been my help.
If my father and mother forsake me,
the Lord will take me up.

Psalm 104 *(part two)*

He makes all things new

All creatures look to you
to give them their food in due season;
when you give to them, they gather it up;
when you open your hand, they are filled with good things.

When you send forth your spirit, they are created;
and you renew the face of the ground.

May the glory of the Lord endure for ever;
may the Lord rejoice in his works –
who looks on the earth and it trembles,
who touches the mountains and they smoke.

I will sing to the Lord as long as I live;
I will sing praise to my God while I have being.
May my meditation be pleasing to him,
for I rejoice in the Lord.

Bless the Lord, O my soul.

Summer – Ordinary Time

Psalm 65 *A song in summer*

Praise is due to you,
O God, in Zion;
and to you shall vows be performed,
O you who answer prayer!
To you all flesh shall come.
When deeds of iniquity overwhelm us,
you forgive our transgressions.
Happy are those whom you choose and bring near
to live in your courts.
We shall be satisfied with the goodness of your house,
your holy temple.

By your strength you established the mountains;
you are girded with might.
You silence the roaring of the seas,
the roaring of their waves,
the tumult of the peoples.
Those who live at earth's farthest bounds are awed by your signs;
you make the gateways of the morning and the evening shout for joy.

You visit the earth and water it,
you greatly enrich it;
the river of God is full of water;
you provide the people with grain,
for so you have prepared it.
You water its furrows abundantly,
settling its ridges,
softening it with showers,
and blessing its growth.
You crown the year with your bounty;
your wagon tracks overflow with richness.
The pastures of the wilderness overflow,
the hills gird themselves with joy,
the meadows clothe themselves with flocks,
the valleys deck themselves with grain,
they shout and sing together for joy.

The Lord is my shepherd, I shall not want.
He makes me lie down in green pastures;
he leads me beside still waters;
he restores my soul.
He leads me in right paths
for his name's sake.

Even though I walk through the darkest valley,
I fear no evil;
for you are with me;
your rod and your staff —
they comfort me.

Psalm 23 *Green pastures*

You prepare a table before me
in the presence of my enemies;
you anoint my head with oil;
my cup overflows.
Surely goodness and mercy shall follow me
all the days of my life,
and I shall dwell in the house of the Lord
my whole life long.

Psalm 33 The counsel of the Lord stands for ever

Rejoice in the Lord, O you righteous.
Praise befits the upright.
Praise the Lord with the lyre;
make melody to him with the harp of ten strings.
Sing to him a new song;
play skilfully on the strings, with loud shouts.

For the word of the Lord is upright,
and all his work is done in faithfulness.
He loves righteousness and justice;
the earth is full of the steadfast love of the Lord.
By the word of the Lord the heavens were made,
and all their host by the breath of his mouth.
He gathered the waters of the sea as in a bottle;
he put the deeps in storehouses.
Let all the earth fear the Lord;
let all the inhabitants of the world stand in awe of him.
For he spoke, and it came to be;
he commanded, and it stood firm.

The Lord brings the counsel of the nations to nothing;
he frustrates the plans of the peoples.
The counsel of the Lord stands for ever,
the thoughts of his heart to all generations.

Our soul waits for the Lord;
he is our help and shield.
Our heart is glad in him,
because we trust in his holy name.
Let your steadfast love, O Lord, be upon us,
even as we hope in you.

I love you, O Lord, my strength.
The Lord is my rock, my fortress, and my deliverer,
my God, my rock in whom I take refuge,
my shield, and the horn of my salvation, my stronghold.
I call upon the Lord, who is worthy to be praised;
so I shall be saved from my enemies.

The cords of death encompassed me;
the torrents of perdition assailed me;
the cords of Sheol entangled me;
the snares of death confronted me.

In my distress I called upon the Lord;
to my God I cried for help.
From his temple he heard my voice,
and my cry to him reached his ears.

He reached down from on high, he took me;
he drew me out of mighty waters.
He delivered me from my strong enemy,
and from those who hated me;
for they were too mighty for me.

They confronted me in the day of my calamity;
but the Lord was my support.
He brought me out into a broad place;
he delivered me, because he delighted in me.

It is you who light my lamp;
the Lord, my God, lights up my darkness.
By you I can crush a troop,
and by my God I can leap over a wall.

You exalted me above my adversaries;
you delivered me from the violent.

For this I will extol you, O Lord, among the nations,
and sing praises to your name.

Psalm 139 *What is man?*

O Lord, you have searched me and known me.
You know when I sit down and when I rise up;
you discern my thoughts from far away.
You search out my path and my lying down,
and are acquainted with all my ways.
Even before a word is on my tongue,
O Lord, you know it completely.
You hem me in, behind and before,
and lay your hand upon me.
Such knowledge is too wonderful for me;
it is so high that I cannot attain it.

Where can I go from your spirit?
Or where can I flee from your presence?
If I ascend to heaven, you are there;
if I make my bed in Sheol, you are there.
If I take the wings of the morning
and settle at the farthest limits of the sea,
even there your hand shall lead me,
 and your right hand shall hold me fast.
If I say, 'Surely the darkness shall cover me,
and the light around me become night',
even the darkness is not dark to you;
the night is as bright as the day,
for darkness is as light to you.

Psalm 139 *continued*

It was you who formed my inward parts;
you knit me together in my mother's womb.
I praise you, for I am fearfully and wonderfully made.
Wonderful are your works;
that I know very well.
My frame was not hidden from you,
when I was being made in secret,
intricately woven in the depths of the earth.
Your eyes beheld my unformed substance

In your book were written
all the days that were formed for me,
when none of them as yet existed.
How weighty to me are your thoughts, O God!
How vast is the sum of them!
I try to count them – they are more than the sand;
I come to the end – I am still with you.

Search me, O God, and know my heart;
test me and know my thoughts.
See if there is any wicked way in me,
and lead me in the way everlasting.

Psalm 127 *If the Lord does not build the House*

Unless the Lord builds the house,
those who build it labour in vain.
Unless the Lord guards the city,
the guard keeps watch in vain.
It is in vain that you rise up early
and go late to rest,
eating the bread of anxious toil;
for he gives sleep to his beloved.

Sons are indeed a heritage from the Lord,
the fruit of the womb a reward.
Like arrows in the hand of a warrior
are the sons of one's youth.
Happy is the man who has
his quiver full of them.
He shall not be put to shame
when he speaks with his enemies in the gate.

Autumn – All Souls – Christ the King

Psalm 51 *Put a steadfast spirit within me*

Have mercy on me, O God,
according to your steadfast love;
according to your abundant mercy
blot out my transgressions.
Wash me thoroughly from my iniquity,
and cleanse me from my sin.

For I know my transgressions,
and my sin is ever before me.
Against you, you alone, have I sinned,
and done what is evil in your sight.
You desire truth in the inward being;
therefore teach me wisdom in my secret heart.
Purge me with hyssop, and I shall be clean;
wash me, and I shall be whiter than snow.
Let me hear joy and gladness;
let the bones that you have crushed rejoice.
Hide your face from my sins,
and blot out all my iniquities.

> Create in me a clean heart, O God,
> and put a new and right spirit within me.
> Do not cast me away from your presence,
> and do not take your holy spirit from me.
> Restore to me the joy of your salvation,
> and sustain in me a willing spirit.

O Lord, open my lips,
and my mouth will declare your praise.
For you have no delight in sacrifice;
if I were to give a burnt-offering, you would not be pleased.
The sacrifice acceptable to God is a broken spirit;
a broken and contrite heart, O God, you will not despise.

Psalm 90 *You sweep us away like a dream*

Lord, you have been our dwelling-place
in all generations.
Before the mountains were brought forth,
or ever you had formed the earth and the world,
from everlasting to everlasting you are God.

You turn us back to dust,
and say, 'Turn back, you mortals.'
For a thousand years in your sight
are like yesterday when it is past,
or like a watch in the night.

You sweep them away; they are like a dream,
like grass that is renewed in the morning;
in the morning it flourishes and is renewed;
in the evening it fades and withers.

For all our days pass away under your wrath;
our years come to an end like a sigh.
The days of our life are seventy years,
or perhaps eighty, if we are strong;
even then their span is only toil and trouble;
they are soon gone, and we fly away.

Psalm 90 *continued*

So teach us to count our days
that we may gain a wise heart.

Satisfy us in the morning with your steadfast love,
so that we may rejoice and be glad all our days.
Make us glad for as many days as you have afflicted us,
and for as many years as we have seen evil.
Let your work be manifest to your servants,
and your glorious power to their children.
Let the favour of the Lord our God be upon us,
and prosper for us the work of our hands—
O prosper the work of our hands!

Psalm 102 *My days are passing like a shadow*

Hear my prayer, O Lord;
let my cry come to you.
Do not hide your face from me
on the day of my distress.
Incline your ear to me;
answer me speedily on the day when I call.

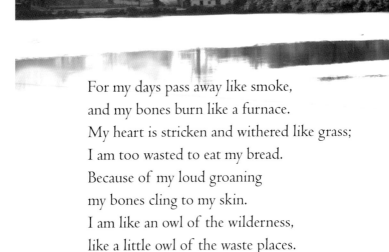

For my days pass away like smoke,
and my bones burn like a furnace.
My heart is stricken and withered like grass;
I am too wasted to eat my bread.
Because of my loud groaning
my bones cling to my skin.
I am like an owl of the wilderness,
like a little owl of the waste places.
I lie awake;
I am like a lonely bird on the housetop.

I eat ashes like bread,
and mingle tears with my drink,
My days are like an evening shadow;
I wither away like grass.

He has broken my strength in mid-course;
he has shortened my days.
'O my God,' I say, 'do not take me away
at the mid-point of my life,
you whose years endure
throughout all generations.'

Long ago you laid the foundation of the earth,
and the heavens are the work of your hands.
They will perish, but you endure;
they will all wear out like a garment.
You change them like clothing, and they pass away;
but you are the same, and your years have no end.

Margaret Henry, see Introduction page 11.

Psalm 121 The Lord is your Guard & your Shade

I lift up my eyes to the hills –
from where will my help come?
My help comes from the Lord,
who made heaven and earth.

He will not let your foot be moved;
he who keeps you will not slumber.
He who keeps Israel
will neither slumber nor sleep.

The Lord is your keeper;
the Lord is your shade at your right hand.
The sun shall not strike you by day,
nor the moon by night.

The Lord will keep you from all evil;
he will keep your life.
The Lord will keep
your going out and your coming in
from this time on and for evermore.

Psalm 91 *His angels keep you*

You who live in the shelter of the Most High,
who abide in the shadow of the Almighty,
will say to the Lord, 'My refuge and my fortress;
my God, in whom I trust.'
For he will deliver you from the snare of the fowler
and from the deadly pestilence;
he will cover you with his pinions,
and under his wings you will find refuge;
his faithfulness is a shield and buckler.
You will not fear the terror of the night,
or the arrow that flies by day,
or the pestilence that stalks in darkness,
or the destruction that wastes at noonday.

A thousand may fall at your side,
ten thousand at your right hand,
but it will not come near you.
You will only look with your eyes
and see the punishment of the wicked.

Because you have made the Lord your refuge,
the Most High your dwelling-place.

Psalm 91 *continued*

No evil shall befall you,
no scourge come near your tent.

For he will command his angels concerning you
to guard you in all your ways.
On their hands they will bear you up,
so that you will not dash your foot against a stone.
You will tread on the lion and the adder,
the young lion and the serpent you will trample under foot.

Those who love me, I will deliver;
I will protect those who know my name.
When they call to me, I will answer them;
I will be with them in trouble,
I will rescue them and honour them.
With long life I will satisfy them,
and show them my salvation.

Psalm 71 *You will give me back my life*

In you, O Lord, I take refuge;
let me never be put to shame.
In your righteousness deliver me and rescue me;
incline your ear to me and save me.
Be to me a rock of refuge,
a strong fortress, to save me,
for you are my rock and my fortress.

For you, O Lord, are my hope,
my trust, O Lord, from my youth.
Upon you I have leaned from my birth;
it was you who took me from my mother's womb.
My praise is continually of you.

Do not cast me off in the time of old age;
do not forsake me when my strength is spent.
For my enemies speak concerning me,
and those who watch for my life consult together.
They say, 'Pursue and seize that person
whom God has forsaken,
for there is no one to deliver.'

O God, do not be far from me;
O my God, make haste to help me!

Psalm 71 *continued*

O God, from my youth you have taught me,
and I still proclaim your wondrous deeds.
So even to old age and grey hairs,
O God, do not forsake me,
until I proclaim your might
to all the generations to come.
Your power and your righteousness, O God,
reach the high heavens.

You who have done great things,
O God, who is like you?
You who have made me see many troubles and calamities
will revive me again;
from the depths of the earth
you will bring me up again.
You will increase my honour,
and comfort me once again.
I will also praise you with the harp
for your faithfulness, O my God;

I will sing praises to you with the lyre,
O Holy One of Israel.
My lips will shout for joy
when I sing praises to you;
my soul also, which you have rescued.

Psalm 30

You have changed my mourning into dancing

I will extol you, O Lord, for you have drawn me up,
and did not let my foes rejoice over me.
O Lord my God, I cried to you for help,
and you have healed me.
O Lord, you brought up my soul from Sheol,
restored me to life from among those gone down to
the Pit.

Sing praises to the Lord, O you his faithful ones,
and give thanks to his holy name.
For his anger is but for a moment;
his favour is for a lifetime.
Weeping may linger for the night,
but joy comes with the morning.

Hear, O Lord, and be gracious to me!
O Lord, be my helper!

You have turned my mourning into dancing;
you have taken off my sackcloth
and clothed me with joy,
so that my soul may praise you and not be silent.
O Lord my God, I will give thanks to you for ever.

Luke 2:29-32 Nunc Dimittis *Go in peace*

Master, now you are dismissing your servant in peace,
according to your word;
for my eyes have seen your salvation,
which you have prepared in the presence of all peoples,
a light for revelation to the Gentiles
and for glory to your people Israel.

Psalm 72 *He shall rule from sea to sea*

Give the king your justice, O God,
and your righteousness to a king's son.
May he judge your people with righteousness,
and your poor with justice.
May the mountains yield prosperity for the people,
and the hills, in righteousness.
May he defend the cause of the poor of the people,
give deliverance to the needy,
and crush the oppressor.

May he live while the sun endures,
and as long as the moon, throughout all generations.

May he be like rain that falls on the mown grass,
like showers that water the earth.
In his days may righteousness flourish
and peace abound, until the moon is no more.

May he have dominion from sea to sea,
and from the River to the ends of the earth.

For he delivers the needy when they call,
the poor and those who have no helper.
He has pity on the weak and the needy,
and saves the lives of the needy.
From oppression and violence he redeems their life;
and precious is their blood in his sight.

Long may he live!
May gold of Sheba be given to him.
May prayer be made for him continually,
and blessings invoked for him all day long.
May there be abundance of grain in the land;
may it wave on the tops of the mountains;
may its fruit be like Lebanon;
and may people blossom in the cities
like the grass of the field.
May his name endure for ever,
his fame continue as long as the sun.
May all nations be blessed in him;
may they pronounce him happy.

Blessed be the Lord, the God of Israel,
who alone does wondrous things.
Blessed be his glorious name for ever;
may his glory fill the whole earth. Amen and Amen.